TWO HEARTS AS ONE

Jesse Wilson

authorHOUSE®

AuthorHouse™
1663 Liberty Drive
Bloomington, IN 47403
www.authorhouse.com
Phone: 1-800-839-8640

First published by AuthorHouse 3/17/2010

ISBN: 978-1-4490-8973-3 (sc)
ISBN: 978-1-4490-8974-0 (e)

Library of Congress Control Number: 2010903481

Printed in the United States of America
Bloomington, Indiana

This book is printed on acid-free paper.

A BURNING RAGE

A burning rage is eating at the very center.
Of my heart and mind just waiting to enter.
My true self and destroy the remnants of what might be.
The dying hope of a heart's shouted plea.

This rage is the bearer of an emotional strain.
Causing within my mind a life draining pain.
This rage is destroying who I am and what I want to be.
It's burning away the wick of hope inside of me.

I'm gradually losing grip of a last crying plea.
Praying for a fair who might have the key.
To the source of this rage which I might confess.
To be the burning destroyer known as loneliness.

JESSE WILSON

A CRY FOR DESIRE

In the early morning's dawn, none stand alone.
But together with pride for a future unknown.
At first awakening you feel the warmth of a fire.
As later through the pain you hear a cry for desire.

Some unknown are the ones who persist.
For drive and patience leaders continually insist.
Push on are the words of old to say.
A cry for desire sounding throughout the day.

To view from afar but yet feel within.
Are the qualities needed for each day to begin.
As hopes and aspirations, like birds, fly higher.
So on and on goes a cry for desire.

CRY OUT WE ALL FOR DESIRE.
KINDLE THE FLAMES OF A DETERMINED FIRE.
JESSE WILSON

A DREAM ALONE

A dream alone is a lonesome soul.
A dream alone serves no goal.
Many a thought has drifted to this.
A dream alone wonders amiss.

A company of compassion, an escort of love.
Can give a dream, something to dream of.
A dream alone walks a narrow path.
But a dream accompanied escapes a lonely wrath.

The source of a dream comes from where?
It can move as secretly as life's purest air.
A breath of understanding, a gasp of respect.
Tis the most desired companion for a dream to detect.

A dream alone steers an uncertain course.
Its much needed compass cannot come from its source.
The deliverance of hope is a gift of faith.
Making sure a dream alone is not a wraith.

JESSE WILSON

A FRIEND

There are those who would define a friend.
As one who stays close until the very end.
Through times of sunshine and times of rain.
A friend is there to share in the pain.

With an open heart and a tight embrace.
A friend is there to bring a smile to your face.
To your heart it means so much.
To feel a kind and tender touch.

When of love your world seems dry.
Go ahead, to a friend and cry.
Let it out, don't lock it within.
A friend is there, with a new life to begin.

You may still hurt when you think of her or him.
But remember your friends, you matter to them.
They are there to hold your hand.
Forming with friendship, a lifelong band.

I know these things because I hurt inside.
From my friends, I try my feelings not to hide.
They pick me up, when I'm feeling down.
They make me smile, when I want to frown.

There are good times to share with others.
With your friends, who are like your brothers.
Laughing and joking and running around.
Feeling so free, as if above the ground.

All this time you may never forget.
You may find a reason, or a regret.
But learn from this and start anew.
There's now a more open life waiting for you.

Sometimes a friend has to cause you pain.
To make you see life and see it plain.
They don't want to do it, but it must be done.
Before a truly open life for you, can be begun.

I see these things more clearly now through the loss of a dream.
Is it truly lost, or does it just that way seem.
I'm confused right now, the answer I'm not sure of.
There's nothing more helpful though, than a good friend's true love.

When it seems that you are sliding back.
A friend is there to put you on the right track.
They tell you what they have told you before.
And it is then that their friendship means even more.

I could go on and on of how to define a friend.
But you will know the truth in the very end.
They'll be there, by your side.
Through thick and thin, there they'll reside.

Thank you all for being there for me.
For helping me see life in this world as a reality.
If ever there is anything i can do.
My true friends know, I'll be there for you.

JESSE WILSON

A HEART SO KIND

At this moment of darkness and despair.
I see in my dreams a most lovely fair.
She has sparkling eyes and a glistening smile.
If only I could see her in reality for just awhile.

She is beautiful and kind.
With a heart not blind.
To my feelings and fears.
Or my sorrows and tears.

In my dreams she always be.
Close by my side to care for me.
Someday I dream to truly find.
The most lovely fair with a heart so kind.

JESSE WILSON

A HEAVENLY FAIR

A heavenly fair does enter my dreams.
Whenever at a beauty to look, my mind does deem.
With her embracing eyes, a smile so bright.
And a figure truly divine.
She could easily have any heart.
I just wish it would be mine.

Of these thoughts I'm sure she is aware.
For she is truly a beautiful and honest fair.
The way she moves tells you everything.
Such gracefulness from such a lovely thing.

The key to my heart I would gladly give.
For my dream in reality to every day live.
A heavenly fair is in my dreams.
And thinking of her is all my mind deems.

JESSE WILSON

A LADY FAIR

Twer born to be a lady fair.
Legends made of men who dare.
True knights of bold these legends say.
On fiery white steeds they ride away.

Adorned in beauty and light colored hair.
A damsel in waiting for a man who would dare.
To be the one which seeks the heart.
Of a lady fair and not to part.

Tall of stature and character too.
This lady fair is truly you.
Though not a knight, I truly dare.
To capture the heart of a lady fair.

I ride no steed of fiery white.
But journey through life with a heart of might.
To be thy knight, ask thee I dare.
For none come close to the lady fair.

TO A LADY FAIR
JESSE WILSON

A LEGEND MAID

A fair, of spoken, no more has been.
Than the one of old in legends has been.
Ransom and wealth of countless amount, has always been paid.
To gain or restore the presence of a legend maid.

Of long dark hair and features divine.
For only one man in every wished what was mine.
Nor mortal man, nor god's desire is stayed.
For the longing to possess the ever such legend maid.
Such a fair these eyes have beheld.
Name of which should not be spelled.
Knights may fall and in minds their memories not stayed.
But always there will be instilled the image of a legend maid.

JESSE WILSON

A LOOK AHEAD

I see the future as I look ahead.
On one side happiness, on the other dread.
Happiness is a dream I've already realized.
Dread is a loss, I hope never to recognize.

I've written "Heaven Sent", "Mi Pedaso Pequeno De Cielo", and "My Dream In life".
About someone special, who in her own way not knowing, helps me deal with toil and strife.
All of these words, I promise are from the heart and true.
My dream in life, they are all meant for you.

I live my life from day to day.
To get through life I know no other way.
I look ahead though, and my dream goes far.
Will my dream see my intentions in life as true, and for what they are.

One link in life has already been completed.
From my heart and mind my dream will never be deleted.
One loss in life I've had to suffer through.
Oh the Lord above, please don't let there be two.

So much I could write, so much I could say.
I will write again of life another day.
I have so much inside of me.
To share with another, who I want so much there to be.

I'LL LIVE DAY BY DAY.
BUT I'LL STILL LOOK AHEAD.
JESSE WILSON

A SINCERE MAN

Sincerity is a quality I like to think I possess.
It's a quality I so truly want to express.
But is there anyone who would dare to span.
The gap of loneliness in the heart of this sincere man.

The pain of loneliness is one that runs so very deep.
At times it hurts so bad inside that my heart begins to weep.
Sincere feelings are the ones I yearn to share the most.
I want even more to find a fair, whose heart to them would be a host.

With sincerity will I find a fair.
With sparkling eyes and lovely hair.
Is there a fair who will tell me I can.
Win her heart because I am a sincere man.

JESSE WILSON

A TRUE FAIR

I see through my eyes, the flowers above.
And then I see you, soft and sweet as a dove.
I think of the beauty that both of you share.
As I gaze into your eyes and at your beautiful brown hair.

Words cannot describe your radiant beauty.
Nor to your enchanting heart do they do a justly deserved duty.
In one man's heart emotions you do stir.
As in a small kitten you would arouse a gentle purr.

You may ask how these words I could write to you.
I only write what I feel is true.
Your heart's obvious beauty is beyond compare.
You are honestly a true and most lovely fair.

JESSE WILSON

A VOICE BID SILENT

A voice bid silent by means not mine.
Tis a voice in a way giving me a sign.
So many words I should wish to speak.
But my heart does hide them, shy and meek.

My heart is telling me to speak them aloud.
But they seem to be suppressed by a fearful shroud.
Tis a chance worth taking, but that is me.
To utter the words for a desire to be.

A voice bid silent to others it seems.
Yet uttered to me whenever it deems.
Shall it speak to one known to care.
Shall it also the thoughts of my heart, share.

I have spoken before and met with pain.
But will silence this time, anything gain.
Only one heart knows what is meant.
When words are uttered by a voice bid silent.

JESSE WILSON

A VOICE OF CHOICE

I'm sitting and listening to my father's voice.
One of experience and one of choice.
Telling me of dreams that may be realized.
Telling me of losses that must be recognized.

He speaks of the life that is mine to live.
And of the many things the world has to give.
Of many opportunities due to education.
Of great attainments provided through dedication.

One choice in life is to care for others.
To treat your friends as if they were your brothers.
To do for others all that you can.
But to remain for yourself your own man.

I care for others each and every day.
But I care for one in a special way.
My father sees a dream that I've lost.
And says it's up to me to determine its cost.

I looked into his eyes as I told of my dream.
I saw in them an uplifting gleam.
If it's what you want, he says, hold on with your heart.
But from your mind don't let reality depart.

I heed his words, his words of life.
Of making choices and dealing with strife.
To get an education and make my life's choice.
Is the main desire in my father's voice.

His is a voice of giving and of giving more.
Leaving open a parental door.
To enter and listen to an experienced voice.
When I find it difficult to make a choice.

I see my father working hard every day.
Dealing with life in his own way.
Making his mark as a man who can do many things.
Accepting from life that which to him it brings.

I'm so proud when I think of you.
I don't say it often enough Dad, but I love you.
I will always listen to my father's voice.
One of experience, and one of choice.

JESSE WILSON

A.K.A. A FAIR UNSEEN

Words exchanged with a fair unseen.
Whose heart and mind to me seem keen.
With unsurpassed beauty that is easy to tell.
And with everlasting enchantment that over any man would weave a spell.

A fair unseen with whom it is easy to converse.
Whose heart and mind share emotions to immerse.
Lovely brown eyes and lovely brown hair.
Go hand-in-hand with the countless qualities of such a lovely fair.

Words exchanged with a fair unseen.
Whose heart emits emotions truly peaceful and serene.
To me, such a fair so lovely and kind.
Is one-in-a-million, not to easy to find.

JESSE WILSON

ALONE AGAIN

Loneliness is setting in.
That same sad feeling is back again.
There's an emptiness inside that I'm afraid to explain.
But I will say this, it's an unwanted pain.

The feeling always seems to be the same for me.
I only wish she would answer my heart's plea.
There's a covering of my heart with a hesitant mist.
Could she possibly feel that I exist.

I wear this loneliness as if it were an iron mask.
If only of my feelings she would ask.
At the moment when she would inquire.
My heart's yearning hope would climb higher and higher.

JESSE WILSON

ANOTHER MORNING

The sun does shine on yet another morning.
Nature's many creations brilliantly adorning.
Awakened by a glimmer, a sun's ray perhaps.
I'm wishing to go back into a dreamy time lapse.

In a dream I'm free, with a freedom not complete.
But yet there in my dreams, for my desires I must compete.
A ray of hope and a glimmer of warning.
The sun does shine on yet another morning.

The comings of the day are never truly known.
Expectancies run high, some are even shown.
A sudden brightness the birds are scorning.
The sun does shine on yet another morning.

If one could make the sun shine where.
One had a hope, one had a care.
This one would make it shine on the.
The only one I want for me.

A choice is made, the truth is spoken.
You feel your heart is but a token.
In any market dreams it could buy.
Your own little sun, in your own little sky.

One thing I know, another I don't.
One I will, and one I won't.
A disappointment comes, because of an ignored warning.
But the sun does shine on yet another morning.

Arise again to see the light.
Shining on dreams, grasp one you might.
Your heart is calling, your soul is mourning.
The sun does shine on yet another morning.

Worries are not a burden to bare.
When you have a hope, a dream, and a care.
On which to fall back when things look bad.
You can dwell upon all the good dreams you've had.

JESSE WILSON

APART FROM TOGETHER

Apart from together success will not heed.
Our desire to be the best, which we so strongly need.
Do we know what drives us through darkness and light.
May it be from within us, an unforeseen might.

Apart from together many are not one.
But rather separate entities with goals not done.
Once joined in pride and fueled by desire.
One's goals may only lead, each higher and higher.

Apart from together, we drift alone.
Traveling through a void, upcomings unknown.
Through that which resembles the worst of weather.
One shall persist, if not apart from together.

AS ONE TOGETHER WE WILL SUCCEED.
APART FROM TOGETHER, TO EVEN TRY WE DO NOT NEED.
JESSE WILSON

AS I AM I

As I look up to the moon, and the stars, and the skies.
None match the beauty that I've found in your eyes.
A wisdom I've found which is hard to come by.
Through you I've discovered as I am I.

A time ago we did not know.
That between our hearts a love would grow.
Such as that of a sister and brother.
Surpassed by none, no one other.

A physical distance between us will rise.
But I will never forget the beauty in your eyes.
I will always remember your warm embrace.
And the uplifting hope of the smile on your face.

As I am I, I often think.
Of the many times I was on the brink.
But then I would realize the love that can be.
Because of the friend you are to me.

It does not mean that a friendship must close.
Because in your life, another you chose.
Because I am not that one, I don't want to be.
The cause of a loss of one so dear to me.

At first I thought of giving this to you.
But I have much more to say before I am through.
So with me, it will stay.
But remember these words in your heart every day.

As I am I and you are you.
To each other we should remain true.
A distance between us does not mean apart.
When with each other we stay in the heart.

Tu esta mi amiga siempre.
To you I am the same I pray.
As I am I, I am on my own.
But I will never again be alone.

I am often down, but never out.
When I have beauty such as you to think about.
That is something I can hold on to.
In the form of the friendship I have with you.

You once told me what I mean to you.
But then you said there was something I must do.
I must love myself before I will find.
That by the dream in my life, I have not been left behind.

So to you I will not say goodbye.
Until we meet again, with freedom fly high.
As I look at a star shining in the sky.
I will think of you, as I am I.

ELLA, IF YOU FEEL THE SAME AND SHARE THE SAME WISH FOR A LIFELONG FRIENDSHIP, COME GIVE ME A HUG.
JESSE WILSON

BORN HIGH ABOVE

Rising above all the rest.
A young mother is searching for the perfect nest.
In which to raise her young, soon to be born.
And against the dangers of life to warn.

On the highest limb stretching out from the cliff.
She finds a spot, among the riff.
She gathers materials and works with speed.
For her young, are this world soon to heed.

She completes their home, a fortress of sorts.
And from this point, the dangers of life she thwarts.
From the eggs life has not yet emerged.
But already in the warmth of their mother, the little ones are submerged.

One shell cracks and then another.
The third one also, and they behold each other.
Of first concern, nourishment is needed.
By leaving her young, this can be heeded.

She leaves the nest, feeling her young ones are secure.
Knowing not that they are to the hawk, a lure.
His grip is closed and a young one lives no more.
If only the mother had known before.

Upon her return she discovers the death.
Part of her life is gone in a breath.
One life over, there are still the other two.
She must with more love and care start anew.

Rising above all the rest.
Had she found the perfect nest.
On the highest limb stretching out from the bluff.
Were the young born high enough.

JESSE WILSON

BRIGHT AND SHINING SUN

My emotions inside are confused and turning.
While agonizingly inside my heart and mind are burning.
I don't know what to do.
But who should I talk to.

My day has darkened and my sun has set.
There are so many things that I'm not sure I should regret.
Will my darkness last in grief?
Or will a brightening star come in relief?

So many things in the mind to think about.
So many sorrows in the heart I'm not without.
Has the darkness just begun?
Or will there be another bright and shining sun?

JESSE WILSON

BUT STILL THERE IS LOVE

The greatest of pains never felt before.
The greatest of pains pressing heart's open door.
I look to the one, the almighty above.
A friend has hurt me but still there is love.

I searched near and far for what my heart wanted.
It seemed I went through hell and remained undaunted.
When life seemed too slow I had to give it a shove.
And then my Savior reminded me, but still there is love.

As parents we know that everything and everyone must change.
Our children remind us of the many facets through which we must range.
From their birth until they can soar like a dove.
We must always assure them, but still there is love.

JESSE WILSON

CARMEN AND JUD

I see a young couple as they sit side by side.
And I wonder what they are feeling inside.
Are they thinking of the things a relationship could bring.
As both rain and sunshine come with spring.

Flowers bloom as does love.
It's something that can be sweet and soft as a dove.
The feelings two people share together.
Can be good or bad, just like a day's weather.

I see a young couple sitting side by side.
And I wonder what they are feeling inside.
Their minds are both swimming in an emotional flood.
I see a young couple Carmen and Jud.

JESSE WILSON

CAUSE FOR CARING

To awaken in the morning to sounds of joy.
Tis the heartfelt wish of a girl and a boy.
Things becoming, meant for sharing.
But still, what is my reason for caring?

There are many reasons that I can think of.
Such as life, liberty, happiness, and love.
Thinking of these reasons may bring our thoughts to a pause.
But we will all discover, that anytime there is caring, there is a cause.

Life may bring us many sorrows and joys.
That are seen so differently through the smiles of little girls and boys.
No matter what fate deals us, as long as we are sharing.
There will always be a cause for caring.

JESSE WILSON

COMMONS

Be off with thy commons you wandering knave.
Wistful visions thou soul can't save.
Round thy burdens and carry them high.
For thou shalt never see the light from the sky.

Dwell within thy pitiful hovel.
Keep at hand thy axe and shovel.
Trod the roads with dirt in the lanes.
For thy commons are not welcome on the well traveled mains.

This beastful voice within thine heart.
Will always be of thee a part.
Until one day thee set thyself free.
And release thy commons to become like me.

JESSE WILSON

CURIOSITY

A sweet smell arises and fills the air.
Your curiosity it perks, and lets you know it's there.
It's a fragrance of roses and all that's good.
The source of the curiosity, see it, you should.

Curiosity is a weapon used against a man's heart.
Its effect has been devastating from the start.
The fragrance gets stronger as the curiosity approaches.
Across the border of your heart it encroaches.

You may have realized the source I have not yet revealed.
But for my heart's sake I will keep it concealed.
Curiosity symbolizes beauty and also grace.
Two of the things, hardest for a man to face.

Of all the possibilities this source could be.
You must know by now Curiosity is She.
Even though revealed there will always be.
The feeling I know as Curiosity.

More than any other Curiosity is a driving force.
It steers a man along an unpredictable course.
Over the hills and through the trees.
He chases after curiosity caused pleas.

There's an old expression "curiosity killed the cat".
Sometimes I do, and then again I don't believe that.
If it were true there would be.
One dead cat, that cat would be me.

No one knows what this cat might think.
As curiosity brings me to the brink.
Enough dealt with old expressions.
Today I deal with new repressions.

Oh my God I can't believe it's happening again.
My mind is wondering to the places it has already been.
Curiosity has caused me again to awake.
But oh Lord I pray, I mustn't make a mistake.

Curiosity causes me to wonder why.
A special person has to cry.
It's not very often that one can see.
So many special qualities through curiosity.

I wonder if it is a possibility.
That curiosity could be made to work for me.
Some say that things will work out.
And then they remind me of the problem they don't have to think about.

As this feeling grows and multiplies.
It causes more and more outreaching cries.
How will the answer come, in what form will it be.
When will I not have to feel this aching curiosity.

I have my friends, who are like my brothers.
These feelings as such, we respect one another's.
Even one who's like a sister to me.
And also the source of much curiosity.

JESSE WILSON

DAMN OPPINIONS

To hell with society and its damn opinions.
Rock and roll has its own dominion.
Satanic messages, maybe in some.
Do we listen to that, not everyone.

A change in the 50's, from the old to the new.
Discrimination for rock, and thus for me and you.
Grab a brew and enter our dominion.
To hell with society and its damn opinion.

Lose your inhibitions and more than that.
But anybody can tell you, rock is where it's at.
Lose a few brain cells, what a loss.
Damn this world, rock's the boss.

JESSE WILSON

DARE I SAY

Dare I say the words I mean.
To a fair so lovely with a wit so keen.
Many a man would be so proud.
But only one will disperse the cloud.

Truth be only the words I speak.
To reach the point on such a peak.
Each word a step to ask I say.
The question that burns, should I may.

Dare I say the words I mean.
The answer I hear, have I already seen.
Should I ask this question though.
Of a "Lady Fair" who would only know.

SHOULD I ASK ???
JESSE WILSON

DAWNS BE GONE

Dawns be gone from a woeful past.
To seek of happiness, I remember not when last.
Brightening seen of morning's glow.
Shed a light for the future to show.

Dawns be gone and usher forth.
Good will and joy from south and north.
Life's direction guided by such.
May be determined by the slightest touch.

Dawns be gone and do not return.
Forever in a heart remembrance will burn.
Forge through darkness, stroll through light.
Dawns be gone but not towards the night.

JESSE WILSON

DAY BY DAY

What's wrong with living day by day?
If it keeps you going on your way.
Will it work, will it last?
Or will it keep you entrapped in the past?

I wake up in the morning to the rising of the sun.
So why of joy and happiness do I seem to see none?
I've got so much to share, so much to say.
But I keep on living day by day.

A smile on the face of a friend, I see.
It means so much, to the real me.
It keeps me going on my way.
As I go through life day by day.

I've got a friend in a lot of pain.
I try to help her, happiness to gain.
So much I could do, so much I could say.
But I'll keep on living day by day.

Happiness can be soft and cuddly, like a Teddy Bear.
When someone for you, wants to be there.
That's one thing I want, is it wrong to say?
While I keep on living day by day.

Letting go is so very hard.
You feel like life has dealt you the lowest card.
You never let go completely, that's why I say.
I'll just keep on living day by day.

My friend says to let my real self show.
I tried that once and life said no.
I haven't to this friend of my true self, I'm not sure I should say.
So I'll continue to live day by day.

I've thought of life and ending it all.
But something inside has kept me standing tall.
I tell others that's not the way.
And I keep on living day by day.

My friend tells me to look for a brighter tomorrow.
Something unique each day instead of a new sorrow.
Maybe there's a purpose meant for me, somewhere along the way.
Maybe someone is meant to keep me from living day by day.

RIGHT NOW I'M LIVING DAY BY DAY. WILL IT ALWAYS BE THIS WAY?
JESSE WILSON

DO SORROWS NEVER END

Locked in a space devoid of room.
A consuming darkness brings an endless gloom.
No broken parts nor wrongs may mend.
Which poses the question, do sorrows never end?

A mighty man, Atlas there was.
Who bore the weight of the world, for mistakes because.
I feel the weight I bare is the same.
Though I can do nothing, nor am I to blame.

Tis a sea of emptiness in storms I face.
Carrying so much weight shall I lose the race.
If hope was the answer, no problem would there be.
Nor would the weight of the world be so heavy on me.

As day by day life goes on.
I begin to wonder, with the coming of dawn.
So many wrongs in matters to tend.
I ask once more, do sorrows never end?

JESSE WILSON

DO WE SEE

My heart has been full of sorrows and fears.
My eyes full of illusions and tears.
What I thought was, was not to be.
There is another, one who is beautiful to see.

Every time I see her, my heart fills with hope.
But then I'm reminded, I'm at the end of emotions rope.
Whenever I see her, she has an enchanting smile.
And I look into her sparkling eyes awhile.

Could it be possible that she might see.
The things I see in her, inside of me.
There's one more question my heart asks with a plea.
That one last question is, do we see?

JESSE WILSON

DREAM CHANCE

Tis a dream a chance, at life and love.
Meant for others or me to think of.
Could it be possible that my true dream.
Could have in her heart, of me a gleam.

She is a dream, a prayer, and a hope.
But with others she has to cope.
When first I spoke to her of this.
Twas a fear in me, that again I would miss.

Yet what founding has such a fear.
Just the thought of her into my eye brings a tear.
In myself I should not find fault.
But rather, the gap between our hearts, with caring vault.

Carla I speak to you as known.
My heart and self to you I've shown.
Material goods, not many I've got.
But my heart and promise, to you, I'd give the lot.

A fool gambles with what might be lost.
But this gamble, my dream, has no cost.
Yes the stakes are high, but the reward guaranteed.
Tis a dream a chance, with something for me to heed.

Others with you, a chance they've got.
But such a chance to me, more truly means a lot.
Things left behind, cause thoughts as they often do.
But when such is done, you may find the real you.

There have been others, but they were only reflections of you.
With such a chance, oh the things I could do.
The happiness and joy I would bring to you.
And into my life a light would shine anew.

A dream is a chance at life and love.
Not meant for others, but me to think of.
Only a chance with you Carla, I ask.
By this I remove my last fear's mask.

JESSE WILSON
IF YOU AGREE CARLA, TAKE MY OTHER HAND.

DREAM PLACE

Now I dream of a certain place.
I don't know where or why.
Now I dream of a certain place.
Will I see it before I die.

Could it be a place meant for me?
To live in eternity.
So much pressure all around.
No, life ain't keeping me down.

Above all else I'll always care.
Above all else I want to share.
So much I have to give.
But in loneliness I'm forced to live.

Now I dream of a certain place.
I don't know where or why.
Now I dream of a certain place.
Will I see it before I die.

The laughter comes from another one.
Who in his life has a rising sun.
She is there but oh!!!
The other one he says let's go slow.

I'm caught in the middle, I'm on the line.
I wish their happiness could be mine.
The part of me that's worth the most.
I no longer gladly boast.

Now I dream of a certain place.
I don't know where or why.
Now I dream of a certain place.
Will I see it before I die.

JESSE WILSON
NOW I DREAM OF A CERTAIN PLACE
WILL I SEE IT BEFORE I DIE

DULCES PARA A DULCE

I see a young beauty with tears in her eyes.
And it brings to me an emotional pain inside.
To her sadness I'm not sure what to say.
But I will say this, she deserves dulces para a dulce.

A shoulder if needed will always be hers.
If ever inside she feels emotional stirs.
It saddens me to see such a beauty cry.
So much so that I want to cry.

I see a most lovely fair with tears in her eyes.
And my feelings tell me she is hurting inside.
To her pain I can say.
You do deserve dulces para a dulce.

JESSE WILSON

EARLY WONDERS

Drifting through my mind as thoughts go asunder.
Such beauty and brightness in early morning wonder.
An early bird's flight is followed by another.
First one leads and then another.

Early shown through light.
Many wonders are within sight.
To reach out and touch, some you may.
But others in sight may be too far away.

At first the sun shows.
What only in light grows.
Touched by the hand of night.
They withdraw from all sight.

As I sit and ponder in an early daze.
The many wonders with the sun's gaze.
As we drift in life and go asunder.
We will always dwell on our early wonders.

JESSE WILSON

ENDLESS WAITING

Is it to be in years to pass.
Or the hours and minutes that so quickly amass.
Something from beyond is curiosity baiting.
While here at heart it seems endless waiting.

Over the horizon or around the bend.
So near to receive, so far to send.
Just beyond the grasp of an outreaching hand.
Yet well within the sight of a heart's demand.

To be such a prize would seem to bare.
A burden unwanted if not to care.
Many things of want, so few of need.
We let our hearts with curiosity lead.

Oh to be in the years to pass.
The hours and minutes are to amass.
If only to find curiosity is baiting.
Would it cease the endless waiting.

JESSE WILSON

ENDLESS WALK

In sleep no rest is taken from.
An endless walk, which beckons, come.
Arise in the morning to set the day's pace.
Though it may seem, life is not a race.

So few and far between.
Are the ranks of a commoner and a king.
The lengthy path to a goal in life.
Seems an endless walk through struggle and strife.

Birth is a first step toward maturity.
All life's aims are at security.
Down life's hall toward the door at the end.
To finish this walk we do intend.

JESSE WILSON

FAITHFUL ONES

Endurance and caring are things required.
Though some not well and others tired.
They may not cry out to show their pain.
But trying to hide it is an effort in vain.

Before the sun's rise they are well prepared.
If only everyone realized just how much they cared.
Not ending early their days go on.
Through toil and trouble until well after dawn.

Trained to help and skilled in aid.
By our side the faithful ones have stayed.
Being strong and stout they are loyal to their duty.
While still remaining figures of beauty.

Being masculine or feminine is not the most important thing.
But to a person in pain, a smile they bring.
Working side by side they pull us through.
To be without them, what could we do.

I myself, of them have favors asked.
And my wants and needs are never passed.
No pain untreated nor job undone.
I speak of the lovely and loyal faithful ones.

TO THOSE WHO ARE ALWAYS THERE WHEN NEEDED LEAVING NO ONES PAIN UNHEADED.
JESSE WILSON

FLY ON MY DREAM

Fly on my dream you have your own life to live.
So many things to this world you give.
Your charm, your beauty, your grace, and your heart.
From my mind these will never depart.

You are my dream Linie and you always will be.
For an open life you've given to me.
All of the things I say I live to do.
I was going against in what I was doing to you.

I hope you will always remember me.
And close to my heart will want to be.
Fly high my dream and take nothing but the best.
I'll always be here for you, with all the rest.

The first time I saw you, you were sitting.
Alone in the corner, while the views were hitting.
My heart and mind, which were suddenly thrust.
Into the realistic image of my dream, in which I was to trust.

With tears in your eyes and your hand on my face.
You said I was a beautiful person and that I'd win life's race.
I thank you for that, and I want you to believe.
That you'll take part of me with you if you leave.

No one else will ever receive.
My deepest caring in which I believe.
If it is ever meant for on the ground you to be.
Land softly my dream and come to me.

**FLY ON ADELINA
DON'T EVER FORGET ME
I'LL ALWAYS LOVE YOU
JESSE WILSON**

FOR ALL HE LIVES

A woman untouched by any mortal man.
Unknown to her husband, part of God's grand plan.
The greatest of gifts through them he would give.
For all the world, our Lord, Christ would live.

To walk the land for but a few years.
To heal the sick, and dry the tears.
To gather lost souls and bring them home.
For no more in sin's darkness were they to roam.

There were many miracles for all to behold.
But through twelve special men, his story has been told.
They went out and to all declared.
With his amazing grace, none could be compared.

Those foolish ones who could just not understand.
They drove nails through his feet, and one through each hand.
They nailed him there to that cross made of wood.
Believing if he was divine, come down he would.

Christ raised his head, for the heavens to see.
And asked "my God, why hast thou forsaken me?".
The Lord God chose his son to give.
So that we may know, for all he lives.

JESSE WILSON
I DEDICATE THIS POEM TO THE LORD AND PRAY THAT IT BE INSTILLED IN THE HEARTS OF HIS CHILDREN.

FOR ME

So much uncertainty inside I see.
So much uncertainty as to what I want for me.
To say this is so hard, I don't know why.
Help me someone, I desperately cry.

I thought I wanted, but now I doubt.
So many things my mind's tossing about.
I want to be a success, I want to be the best.
But deep inside, I feel I don't know the rest.

I'm sitting here listening to my father's voice.
One of experience and one of choice.
Success is being happy with what you've done.
Then to others, you can be number one.

Mom says I'm her baby, and she'll always be proud.
I hear her voice also, clear and loud.
Sometimes I want so much for her to put her arms around me.
So safe in a world with Mama, so safe I used to be.

Roland says he knows I haven't stopped dreaming.
But he hasn't seen, from my eyes the tears streaming.
John says I don't want to give it what It'll take.
He's right now, but is time off a mistake?

Ella says I have to first love me.
Maybe part of that is doing what I want for me.
One thing I know, is that I need some time.
For me is the inspiration to write this rhyme.

I'm still not certain whether I'm wrong or wright.
But obtain the answer, from others I might.
But one decision made, there will have to be.
Is what's wrong or wright, and what I truly want for me.

WHAT DO I WANT FOR ME?
JESSE WILSON

FORTUNES TELL

Fortunes tell of its coming forth.
Tis a might from the south or a force from the north.
Secrets are to be and divulgence none.
But upon its arrival, our days are done.

Tis hush to speak of such a thought.
Yet its causes and consequences we are taught.
This glorious land will be no more.
If no soul cares to open the door.

The sun's warming glow and the moon's sparkling light.
Will forever be replaced by and endless night.
No more air to breathe or flowers to smell.
Will it come about? only fortunes tell.

JESSE WILSON

FRIENDSHIP

Friendship to me is of value most.
Because inside me, my heart is its host.
It lifts a soul out of the darkest times.
While inside the heart creates joyous chimes.

It's a cure for many a problem and many a pain.
Showing a persons feelings are not in vain.
It's the bearer of mercies and good tidings.
From within a soul bringing out its hidings.

Thank you to all those who are friends to me.
Answering with kindness my heart's shouted plea.
If it were not for you, I would not share.
My feelings with those who truly do care.

JESSE WILSON

GOALS

A goal not achieved serves as no reason to grieve.
Another attempt can be successful, as long as in yourself you believe.
As long as your best you have always been giving.
There will be many more goals in life meant for your living.

Try try again as the old saying goes.
What achievements for you wait, only God knows.
Just over every horizon, just around every turn.
The light of a lifetime goal does ever beckoning burn.

A lot of people have sacrificed so my life's goals could be achieved.
Many people have cried with me when a goal was not achieved.
Some of my pressures have not been relieved.
God bless you my family and thank you my friends, and I still believe.

JESSE WILSON

GRASPING A DREAM

To myself I do bring pain.
Trying from a dream attention to gain.
My dream you are right, as to the source.
But do you know the reasons for my emotional course.

Guilt I have caused you, but I want that not to be.
For if the guilt should fall, it should fall on me.
Pressures of your own you have to mind.
Relief of mine, is it fair for me to ask of you to find.

The first time I saw you, I knew it then.
You are the dream, that in my mind has always been.
Is it wrong to want attention there to be.
Just a little attention, just a little something for me.

I want, is the hardest thing in the world for me to say.
Because nothing more than doing for others, brings me a brighter day.
Not in return for things I've done, do I want this attention.
But rather it is just a little something in life I want and feel I should mention.

To speak of this in that place, I feel inhibited.
My thoughts there to express, by guilt are prohibited.
So many friends are there for you.
And keeping you from them, was not what I wanted to do.

Remember how happy we were when we first started seeing each other.
Good times, smiles, and friendship: were things we shared with one another.
The first night we talked, expressing what was truly inside.
Holding you in my arms, meant our feelings we didn't have to hide.

If we could ever be that happy again it would mean the world to me.
Being around you brings so much happiness to me.
Adelina your true beauty, both inner and outer, does show so much.
Could a dream come true and our open hearts touch.

JESSE WILSON

HAPPINESS AGAIN

A strange feeling inside hurt me again.
It was so hard to let this feeling in.
This feeling I haven't felt in so long.
Is it right, or is it wrong.

Happiness again, with it I'm not sure how to deal.
Is it imaginary, could it be real.
Happiness again, what do these words mean.
As to their truth it remains to be seen.

JESSE WILSON

HAPPINESS MORROW

Despite today's sadness, trials, and sorrow.
One must always look onward to the happiness of morrow.
Is to be a problem today.
A solution to find, morrow's way.

For what do we search, for what do we strive.
To be the best, or to be alive.
A love not had, or one just lost.
Happiness may be morrow's cost.

The past is behind, the present is now.
Find happiness morrow, we wonder how.
Time not considered in the rhelm of emotion.
To happiness morrow we owe our devotion.

The location of happiness has long been hidden.
In search of this, many miles have been ridden.
Through the mountains and vallies we have been.
But to find morrow's happiness, just look within.

Hidden or not, seek yet we do.
We behave as if it is a concept anew.
Burden or treasure morrow's happiness could be.
To have it would be the latter for me.

The sky may darken causing the light to dim.
And chances of happiness may look mighty grim.
From experience in life we continually borrow.
The belief that there will always be happiness morrow.

JESSE WILSON

HEART OF WILL

Oh misty Earth bring forth thime charms.
Spew forth your demons and your harms.
Into the lives of the innocent you spill.
But you cannot defeat a heart of will.

Mine is one and her's is too.
Her's is a heart of will I say to you.
What may be the good and what may be the bad.
Can both be taken, can both be had.

A bond is made when hearts come together.
Lasting through both calm and stormy weather.
I feel a bond with someone who is so special to me.
Such a bond exists, between She and me.

The will of one might withstand some stormy weather.
But the will of two will last forever.
Brought together will is an unbeatable force.
Guiding its carriers through life's course.

A demon in life confronted will meet defeat.
Truth will prevail and not deceit.
Among the forces of honesty and caring.
Lives are mingled and fulfilled through sharing.

Oh misty Earth I say again.
A heart of will, will defeat thine sin.
In the end the truth will be shown.
The prevailing victor, a heart of will, shll be known.

No matter what you know the truth is inside.
Always willing to reveal, never to hide.
Inside our hearts, love there is still.
I say once again, tis a heart of will.

JESSE WILSON
NO MATTER WHAT, YOU KNOW THE TRUTH AND OTHERS DO ALSO.
BELIEVE IT YOURSELF AND THEY WILL BELIEVE IN YOU.
THE TRUTH WILL ALWAYS REMAIN STRONG IN A HEART OF WILL.

HEAVEN SENT

An angel of beauty, an angel of grace.
With her arms around me brings a smile to my face.
My heart is filled with true intent.
I know in a dream world of reality, she is heaven sent.

Above all thoughts, above all cares.
Happiness with an angel this man shares.
When I'm feeling down, or when I'm feeling blue.
My heaven sent angel, I look to you.

No mortal rose such beauty does possess.
But this heaven sent angel much beauty does address.
Wearing no halo, boasting no wings.
This angel's mere presence causes heart bells to ring.

Meaning not as much to me are my thoughts, feelings, or pains.
As long as by any of them, happiness the angel gains.
This angel is human, normal yes it's true.
My heart will always be open angel, open Adelina for you.

So much to feel good about this angel does convey.
Bringing to my heart and mind a much brighter and open day.
An angel of beauty and grace, what can a mortal man do.
To bring happiness and fulfillment, things of worth in life, unselfishly to you.

Things that make this angel happy are music, friends, and good times.
These are the things that inspire me to make my verses rhyme.
Many things in life do on a soul make an enjoyable demand.
But none more than an open heart and the feel of an outreaching hand.

Compared to a rose this angel I've already done.
As expressed before, true comparisons are none.
The most important quality this angel does possess.
Is an inner beauty so easy to sense and address.

This angel's name is Adelina, yes she's human, it's true.
An angel of beauty, an angel of grace, Adelina I write to you.
With endless writings of this angel, I could truly be content.
Of one thing I will always be convinced, this angel is heaven sent.

JESSE WILSON

I ALWAYS KNEW LOVE

I always knew love when Mom was there.
In her arms, not a fear nor care.
Thru a disappointment or just because.
I always knew, love there was.

A silent cry, she thought not heard.
Not a complaint, not a word.
Yet for me to cry out with pain or fears.
Mom was there to wipe away the tears.

Upon our mother everyone seems to depend.
With our father, a vow until the end.
Always together and never apart.
This family will not end but always start.

I always knew I was not the same.
As the other children playing the game.
But to my mother I was special and unique.
I always knew love, I had not to seek.

A bump or a bruise, a nick or a scratch.
Love was what she used to patch.
A pain or fear, a sorrow or joy.
Mom was there with love to employ.

When all seemed lost, no hope in sight.
That's when Mom's Love showed its might.
A sibling adrift, a cause for a tear.
Thru Mother's love all was seen clear.

Always giving and never to take.
Always willing, my life easier to make.
Not as often felt as when I was a child.
But oh Mother's touch, so tender and mild.

As an infant I crawled, as a child I walked.
Mother remembers the first time I talked.
Always striving for knowledge I know.
Mom was there to watch me grow.

Mother means love, mother means care.
All my successes I want to share.
Something done right, a reward was dealt.
Something done wrong, a firm hand I felt.

So many things I want to say Mom, so many I want to do.
But none more important than my love for you.
I will always believe she was sent from up above.
Because, as you know by now, I always knew love.

JESSE WILSON
I LOVE YOU MOM

I STILL CARE

Life has thrust some cutting blows.
At my heart, because it chose.
To care for someone who doesn't understand.
That what I'm offering is my heart's helping hand.

Life can deliver all it wants.
Its cutting blows, Its agonizing taunts.
With others I'll continue to share.
About others, especially one, I still care.

I still care, I tell my friends.
Even when she brings me to emotional ends.
Every day I make my presence known.
To a dream whose kindness is always shown.

Her harsh words hurt, they truly do.
But the pain is lessened when I remember the words I used to hear from you.
Her heart breaking laugh cuts even deeper.
Flashing through my mind I see the grim reaper.

Her heart is filled with kindness, I know it's there.
I look in your eyes and I know you care.
To acknowledge my presence when I know you feel.
That with me and my ways right now you can't deal.

I know this feeling will always be.
The most important thing inside of me.
With others, especially you, I always want to share.
And I pray with my last words I can say, I still care.

JESSE WILSON

I SWEAR

When work got to be to much
And his health suffered
I told him I loved him
And would always stand by him
Then I suggested that he return to Texas
While our daughter and I stayed with my mom
We talked it over for several days
Before finally deciding to give it a try
We started making plans
With his family and mine
Then one day he was leaving
And I was not
Since then I have seen him twice
In almost two months
It is not nearly enough
But I know it must be
For now

Many times I have cried at night
And also during the day
It is so very hard
With him so far away
Sometimes I wish
It didn't have to be this way
But I know it is for the best
His health is better
His job is better
And when we are together again
Our life will be better
Our love will be stronger
Because of what we've been through
I hope we never have to do this again
Because I don't know if I can
I love and miss him so much
I hate to be apart

Jesse, you will always have my love
My support, my prayers,
My strength, my promises,
My heart, my soul,
And my body
No one could ever take your place
No one could ever take my love away from you
I will stand beside you and love you

Till the end of time
I will never love another
Never as much as I love you
I will bear your children
And raise them with love
I will never leave you
Until the day I die
I love you for always and forever
I SWEAR

TO MY ONE AND ONLY LOVE
JESSE DEAN WILSON
I LOVE YOU
FOR ALWAYS AND FOREVER
I SWEAR !
LOVE ALWAYS,
YOUR WIFE,
PEGGY JEAN WILSON

I WILL NOT KNOW DEFEAT

I will not know defeat.
With the pressures of life clawing at my feet.
When at an instance they think I will fall.
I rise again, and by damn I walk tall.

I will not know defeat, I will rise to the top.
I will only know continue, never know stop.
More and more seem to attack each day.
But in my stance, firm I stay.

My father before me has done the same.
I am proud to carry on with his name.
He would pick me up when I would fall.
Remember my son, you must walk tall.

In trouble now but not down and out.
She believes in me, without a doubt.
With her belief by my side.
Victory from me cannot hide.

Through the darkness a light does shine.
Could this light truly be mine?
Thinking to do, hearts to search.
Upon the decision my dreams do perch.

I pray to the Lord, in whom I trust.
Hear my prayers I know he must.
On my knees, I speak from the heart.
Of my life, he has always been a part.

I will not know defeat.
Because of honesty, not deceit.
The truth will prevail as it has always been said.
I will believe in this until the day I am dead.

Feelings of anger, founded or not.
Are better felt, when forgot.
Indecision as for me or another.
My heart and a guarantee will join us, one another.

Hard work and determination are not all.
That are needed to make the mightiest of men walk tall.
With the pressures of life clawing at my feet.
Only your heart Ella, can keep me from defeat.

YOU ARE MY VICTORY ELLA. I WILL NOT KNOW DEFEAT.
JESSE WILSON

INNOCENCE SCORNED

A vail of blue to the morning eye.
Lit but dimly by a half risen sun.
Expectations are such and running high.
Only to be denied when the light shines fully through.
Niaevity with the sun is risen and born.
Only to reveal an innocence scorned.

The morning's rays become noontime shine.
And a dim indication to the contrary dwindles.
With your day underway and tasks at hand.
Many confusions cloud your mind and heart.
Time is lost and expectations too.
Lost or found innocence is still scorned.

The vail darkens and the sun begins to set.
But the darkness cannot hide what has been revealed.
You wonder in thought as to why you saw.
Your expectations coming true as the day was clear.
A vail of blue to the morning eye.
Bears no thought of an innocence scorned.

JESSE WILSON

LA NINA BONITA

La nina bonita fits her well.
Over one man she weaves an enchanting spell.
The sadness in his heart she does cast away.
With her radiant smile creating a brighter day.

A more lovely rose there has never been.
With an open heart he hopes to win.
With his true feelings and not deceit.
He would oh so tenderly sweep her off her feet.

She's like a dove with gracefulness.
Who has no rival to surpass her loveliness.
Over this man she weaves an enchanting spell.
La nina bonita fits her well.

JESSE WILSON

LAST GAME OF THE SEASON

Last game of the season, it's up for grabs.
So TCB Friday and don't get the crabs.
A victory for effort is what we deserve.
Or an ass kicking from Mac is on reserve.

Keenum says to play hard and keep your cool.
And stop standing around playing pocket pool.
Roemish says to keep your hands up for the pass.
Come on fellas, don't be a dumb ass.

The greatest of athletes and king of DB's.
Gets a joy out of life when a receiver is on his knees.
Tall dark and whatever is coach Modesty.
The coolest of cool in all honesty.

Last game of the season, are we ready?
Our mind and our body must be kept steady.
No pain no gain, no bump no bruise.
So join the GA's and me in saying dump the Roos.

JESSE WILSON

LOOK NOT TO THE PAST

Look not to the past, for it is days gone by.
The sun shines on the future in the morning sky.
Be it a love lost, life's depart.
Wash the tears away with one from the heart.

When your heart fills with anger, and your mind seems lost.
Look to another, for happiness is not the cost.
Words of wisdom and truth to say.
I have as such for each lonely day.

Risk is one that comes with caring.
Look to another whose goal is sharing.
Clinging to the past will not to your dreams lead.
Grasp the future for only to succeed.

Hard times are common, but need not come with frequence.
For trust and caring will follow in their sequence.
Life is a cycle of ups and downs.
Expressed in turn with smiles and frowns.

A journey in life, your heart must take.
Your soul must accompany for its destination to make.
The ticket for this journey need not cost a cent.
Words felt in the heart are words said and meant.

Look not to the past for it is days gone by.
Greet each morning with a new gleam in your eye.
These words I write are of wisdom and true.
Go forth thru the hard times with a perspective anew.

JESSE WILSON

LOSSES FROM THE HEART

Feelings of the heart are so sad to lose.
Of the most value to me are emotional truths.
If confused of your feelings from within.
Look to an open heart, that is where to begin.

As for me other's feelings mean so much.
I believe it is meant for open hearts to touch.
Trust, caring, and love are the three emotions most.
For an open heart to unselfishly host.

I wish nothing in return to be there.
But I ask a question concerning a fair.
Dose what's inside truly count.
To share with others for an unrestrained amount.

JESSE WILSON

LOVE IS WHAT'S NOT

Love is what's not.
Not what shouldn't, but what ought.
So many wants, but not many haves for me.
The only thing in life is my love for Valarie.

Too many times my words I do not utter.
My heart and mind strain, but all is in a flutter.
Love is not as a north wind blows cold.
But more kin to a fire, raging and bold.

Love is not a tiger, but a kitten in play.
Love is not leaving, but wanting to stay.
Love is not dark, as the sky without stars.
It should provide happy memories and not painful scars.

Love is what's not.
But rather what ought.
So many desires and wants for me.
But the only one of worth is my true Valarie.

JESSE WILSON

LOVE YOURSELF

A friend came by last night and asked me to go for a ride.
I did not know that by the end of the night I wouldn't have a problem to hide.
We laughed and we sang and we had a good time.
She gave me the inspiration to write this rhyme.

She said love yourself and others will too.
To be loved, you have to first love you.
Sharing with others means so much to me.
Sharing my love for myself, may just be the key.

It's going to be hard, but I'll give it a try.
If I love myself someone will answer the cry.
I still have the want of someone by my side.
But it feels so much better, this problem not to hide.

The sun is rising and soon the flowers will bloom.
I can put behind me some of the gloom.
There must be something special about a friend.
Who, in little time at all, can bring a problem to an end.

Thank you Ella for being a friend to me.
And providing for the door, the long needed key.
Now all that's left is for me to open the door.
To love myself, and hide no more.

JESSE WILSON

LOVING CARE

My whole life's in front of me now.
It's reality from day to day.
Many people have wondered, they've wondered how?
That throughout my life, I've found the way.

Loving care is the answer I give.
It's the only one that's true.
All throughout this life we live.
Loving care and hard work will find the way for you.

My whole life's in front of me now.
And yes the reality is true.
But for all of those who are wondering how.
With love you'll find your way through.

JESSE WILSON

MI PEDASO PEQUENO DE CIELO

Mi pedaso pequeno de cielo.
My little piece of heaven, wearing no halo.
Qualities of an angel she does possess.
With heavenly beauty and an open heart to address.

A dream to my heart, help has not refused.
When I needed someone, when I was confused.
My life's dream she is, I must be bold.
Don't ever give up, my heart is told.

She symbolizes to me a rising sun.
Rivals on earth, she has none.
Confidence in myself, she has given to me.
Whatever I will, is what I'll be.

To give to her my heart I could.
If ever possible, accept it she would.
No matter what material gains in life I live.
My heart will always be the most important thing I have to give.

To Mi Pedaso Pequeno de Cielo could such an earthly heart be of value.
If it is, or ever could be, I willingly give it to you.
Any man you could hold in a trance.
Would you consider giving this one a chance.

The feelings I have inside.
Are confusing, not easy to hide.
I truly want the angel to have wings.
But sometimes when she flies my heart really stings.

If ever it is possible that she should feel.
The warmth in my heart, to know she is my dream, and it's real.
I would be on a high that could not be brought down.
Nor could I find for life another frown.

I have a fear inside, I must confess.
This agonizing fear, I must address.
You say I'm enough, but is it true.
To myself I'm only enough, if I could mean something to you.

I'm sitting here thinking of all the things I wish I could do.
I see all of the things another can and does do for you.
I'm trying to stand on my own two feet.
I will not give in, nor acknowledge defeat.

Every morning when I pass the place.
I close my eyes, and I see your face.
Every night as I lay my head down to rest.
I see the most beautiful thing on the earth, Adelina your the best.

Knowing not how to sew, I could not mend.
Oh Lord please not like the song, are my dreams meant to be "Dust In The Wind".
When I heard the song, I started to cry.
Knowing inside, I won't let my dream die.

I've lost one dream, I will not lose another.
Another loss, I will not let my life smother.
I have many faults that I'm trying to correct.
But all at once, manhood I can not erect.

Mi Pedaso Pequeno de Cielo.
My little piece of heaven, wearing no halo.
Would you consider giving a country boy a chance.
Who wants nothing more than your life to enhance.

JESSE WILSON
THIS POEM I DEDICATE TO SOMEONE VERY SPECIAL TO ME.
ADELINA MORENO
MI PEDASO PEQUENO DE CIELO

MY DREAM IN LIFE

All my life I've had this dream.
In my mind it has been a glowing beam.
In my heart it has been a source of hope, desire, and drive.
Many times to keep me alive.

All my life I've known she'd come along.
The fair so true, who in my dream does belong.
With boundless beauty, both inside and out.
She would be the one I was never to stop dreaming about.

She is a heavenly figure who could bring any man to his knee.
But I see in my dream, her walking side by side with me.
Our hands are joined and feelings are flowing through.
From my heart to her's, saying I care for you.

In my dream she does return.
The feelings within me, that will ever burn.
In the moonlight, we walk along a trail.
Past the troubles of life, never to fail.

Up until now, fairs in my life have not aroused the dream.
But I knew it then, the first time I saw you, you were shown by the glowing beam.
Shown so bright and shown so clear.
It's hard to believe, that in reality you are so near.

I realized this before words were spoken.
Between us, a bond cannot be broken.
It means so much in my life.
Helping me deal with the toil and strife.

You have been the most special of friends to me.
Answering many times an unspoken plea.
For a hand to hold, a shoulder to lean on.
Life would be over if this were gone.

The things I've done, I realize now.
As bad as it hurts, to correct them I know how.
If you care for someone, give them wings.
And pray for you both, happiness life brings.

Patience and persistence are two virtues in one.
I will use them both to get things done.
I know my dream to be undoubtedly true.
I know my dream Adelina, will always be you.

Others in life, have caused within you a hurt so deep.
I can see this so clearly, and I just want to weep.
I'm afraid this has made you not dare.
To let someone be close, who honestly does care.

I guess now's the time to distinguish the feelings inside.
Those which I've tried so long, for your benefit to hide.
You say to live for myself, because I expect things in return.
Living for myself means doing for others, I need nothing in return.

I care for you and have told you this before.
These feelings I cannot hide, because they've unlocked a door.
They've given me confidence in life, to deal with what may come along.
But always in my dream in life, Adelina you'll belong.

TO MY DREAM IN LIFE, FOR WHOM I CARE.
ADELINA MORENO
BY JESSE WILSON

MY FEARS AND DREAM

Oh Lord please help me, I'm afraid I'm falling.
Into a pit of fear, is it destiny calling.
Of loneliness, another day in my life I could not stand.
An unwanted feeling of insecurity is constantly at hand.

Every day I see a hope and a dream.
And into my heart shines chance's gleam.
A tear in a dream's eye brings the same to me.
But still does not subside the fear in me.

A dream says to me, a beautiful person you are.
As a person, you have what it takes to go far.
All of this, I can visualize.
But if another day of loneliness comes, none I would want to realize.

If it is for a golden heart a dream is searching.
Inside of me, mine is willingly perching.
Whenever music helps a dream, sadness to avoid.
It helps fill in my heart an agonizing void.

Symbols in this world remind me of what I'm afraid is the truth.
I see in the mirror a repulsive youth.
I lash out in fear at every such symbol I see.
Because all that keeps me going is a dream's feelings about me.

Sitting here writing, all the while I see.
A dream in the moonlight, walking with me.
Many say dreams are never to be.
But I have held a dream in reality.

Soft words, tender hugs, and gentle kisses let me know life is worth living for.
But if another moment of loneliness creeps in, life would not be worth living anymore.
A lot I'm not, so much I want to be.
To seem as a man to others, to seem as a man to me.

This good old music brings the dream to my mind.
The right key to the dream's happiness I try so hard to find.
A more beautiful dream there has never been.
Without the dream I could not keep loneliness from coming in.

Standing there, gazing into the eyes.
Of the most beautiful dream, the Lord could devise.
While at the door of my heart the fear of loneliness does pry.
I'm still painfully hoping the dream could answer my cry.

JESSE WILSON

MY HEART STILL PLEAS

My heart still painfully pleas.
For that lovely fair to bring its emptiness to its knees.
This lingering emptiness makes me feel so sad.
Oh why, why does it hurt so bad?

I can't bring myself to tell the most lovely fair.
Of the feelings in my heart that are most certainly there.
If only there were some way these feelings not to hide.
This heartbreaking emptiness might withdraw from inside.

If only I could see a glimmer or a chance.
There might be a way my heart she could enhance.
Until this emptiness is brought to its knees.
My heart still cries out with its beckoning pleas.

JESSE WILSON

MY ONE TRUE LOVE

I used to wish on the stars above
For my one and only true love.
Then I decided that was the wrong one,
It was not a star I should wish upon.
So I prayed to the Lord up above,
To send me someone special to love.
I prayed every night,
For someone just right.
I asked him to help me know,
When that special man would show.

As I was collecting autographs one night,
I saw a most beautiful sight.
At a volunteer fire station,
In a central Texas location,
I saw a handsome man, who stopped my heart.
I had a feeling we would never part.
That night we talked, and my number he took,
It seemed both of us wanted another look.
The next night he called, then came over to talk,
And night after night, he took me for a walk.

For a whole month we met each day,
Always finding something more to say.
Often deserted my Grandmother would seem,
When with this special man I would talk and dream.
I will never forget the day that we met,
The sixth of December will be special yet.
Nineteen-ninety three was the year,
That will always be so very dear.
The best Christmas of my life,
When I wished to be his wife.

Jesse Dean Wilson is his name,
And he wished for mine to be the same.
Proposing with a poem written from his heart,
He offered me all of his life for a start.
I was so happy I started to cry,
With so many tears flowing from my eyes.
My answer I almost forgot to say,
The yes I gave him still stands this very day.
Twas the sixth of January this time,
When I said the yes that would make him mine.

The eighth of May would be our special day,
In nineteen-ninety four there could be no better way.
The wedding was small, just family and friends,
But still it was a day that almost could not end.
Stephenville, Texas was our first home,
But soon we would have to roam.
In search of a better job for our own,
We soon headed to my home town.
Harper, Kansas we stayed for a time,
And had something truly divine.

A precious daughter was born unto us alive,
The twenty-ninth of June Nineteen-ninety five.
She gives us great joy and happiness,
Like none in the world, she could do no less.
Danielle Nicole is her name,
Of course the Wilson is the same.
Someday more children there will be,
And no mother so happy as me.
My love for my family and my life,
Will keep me strong through the strife.

I no longer wish on the stars above,
For I have found my one true love.
By your side I will always be,
My love you will always see.
If ever you leave,
I will forever grieve.
Together we will always stay,
No matter what life sends our way.
Jesse Wilson you will always be,
The one and only man for me.

I LOVE YOU FOREVER!
MY HUSBAND FOR ALWAYS AND FOREVER!
YOUR LOVING WIFE,
PEGGY JEAN WILSON

MY TRUE DREAM

She says I'm Mr. Special.
To me she is also so very special.
When I look upon her picture, into my eyes come a tear and a gleam.
Because I realize what I'm look at is my only true dream.

A more beautiful dream there has never been.
When dwelling upon her beauty, I know just where to begin.
Her open heart is the unrivaled source.
That guides my dream upon its wishful course.

She is the loveliest rose in the garden alive.
Who instills in me a reason to strive.
Carla, the only thing greater than a dream, that I wish you could be for me.
Is the only thing greater that ever there could be, my true reality.

JESSE WILSON

NEED NOT WONDER

All the questions of life and death.
You contemplate as you take each breath.
Pursuing these answers, we sometimes go asunder.
But his word does tell and you need not wonder.

Why would one give his life for all.
And one city stands while another will fall.
Why to our hearts, do we hold some things dear.
All through his word, is made to us clear.

I, myself, may sometimes be found.
Looking towards the heavens while standing on the ground.
Send down the rain, and follow it with thunder.
As to my salvation from this world, I need not wonder.

JESSE WILSON
IN HIS NAME
&
TO HIS GLORY

NIGHT OF THOUGHT

Tis a calming night which has been set forth.
A nearly still breeze blows from the north.
The many changes night has brought.
Make ever lifting this night of thought.

With wondrous hope, I look to the sky.
Yet it answers only with a solemn sigh.
Tis the question I ask, one in vain.
Or the answer to such, a secret to remain.

The source of thought is only to me known.
Yet the search for answers has vastly grown.
Tis like a path with no end in sight.
Yet to travel its length, is destiny's might.

A time unending in thought I've spent.
My mind has wondered and many places went.
To find the answer, the search is ought.
Though seemingly endless through this night of thought.

JESSE WILSON

OF HAPPINESS I SHOULD WRITE

She once said, of happiness I should write.
As in my eyes the moon shines bright.
Many depressed feelings are locked inside.
But much more by the happy ones, would I wish to abide.

Perhaps there is happiness to write about.
Like the people who care, that I can't do without.
There are happy things that my heart hasn't missed.
Like my first lovely fair, and her first sweet kiss.

The happiness does feel better inside of me.
But there is still my heart's shouted plea.
She once said of happiness I should write.
As it is in my eyes, she does shine bright.

JESSE WILSON

ON MY MIND

Dark is the sorrow that often clouds the heart.
Bright is the smile that helps it to depart.
Out of this world there is one of a kind.
And that very one is on my mind.

As I travel down the path of life.
I seem to encounter so much struggle and strife.
Around the next corner or over the hill.
I seem to encounter more, but I can't sit still.

All of these sorrows do battle with joy.
For can one win over with the other one's ploy.
The war rages on as time goes by.
Victory or defeat come only with a sigh.

A thought there dwells within the clouds.
As a storm moves in and the sunlight shrouds.
The Lord brings calm the very next day.
It is for us to know that it is his way.

No halo is worn nor wings with which to fly.
But thoughts of this one do fill the sky.
In all the world she is one of a kind.
And I want her to know an Angel is on my mind.

JESSE WILSON

ONLY ONE

There is only one to speak my heart.
And ask the question from which to start.
There is only one who may reply.
And put at ease, a lasting cry.

A fear of asking I've often had.
Answers have caused my heart to clad.
Itself in armour, much as a shell.
The answer of a fair, only to tell.

There is only one to unlock the door.
And only one to set sail from shore.
On a journey through life, which may not be done.
Until the end cometh, to only one.

JESSE WILSON
THERE IS ONLY ONE

PAIN DRENCHED HEART

My heart is painfully yearning.
And inside emotions are burning.
Yearning for a fair so lovely and understanding.
Who of my pain drenched heart would be undemanding.

The pain seems everlasting.
Like a miner's continual blasting.
Oh when will it cease?
When will there be peace?

The pain and yearning will cease in my heart.
When of my life becomes a part.
The fair so lovely, so kind and understanding.
Who of my pain drenched heart would be undemanding.

JESSE WILSON

POISED FOR GLORY

Take heed all ears for I tell the story.
Of an embattled group poised for glory.
Taking the field at the crack of dawn.
In each heart and mind the passion rages on.

Countless hours of strategy and planning.
Each one has his own station to be manning.
Fight on the run our leader yells.
But ready yourself for the attack he tells.

Through many days and as many nights.
We prepare ourselves for all sounds and sights.
Not jumping at shadows but only what's real.
Before our force all others will kneel.

Time is lessening before the battle to come.
It spells the beginning and end for some.
Through fanatical effort and perfect execution.
We will gain all rewards and allow no retribution.

When our men shall fall there are those who will come.
To help them up and get them back on the run.
This is only a part of the full length story.
About an embattled group poised for glory.

JESSE WILSON

POWER DETERMINED

In a blaze of light a power is felt.
When darkness falls the blow is dealt.
The object falls beneath the blow.
The reason for such we do not know.

We have all felt the power, we have all struck the blow.
With life as the object we will never know.
The reason for the blow nor the source of power.
But we will determine the fatal hour.

If ever we answer the question we ask.
We shall have achieved an impossible task.
In a blaze of light power is felt.
Only you can determine if the blow is to be dealt.

JESSE WILSON
ONLY YOU HOLD THE POWER

PRETENSE TO LIFE

Oh for the sake of pretense to be.
A rich man's cry is a poor man's glee.
The life one leads, the other hates.
The joy one shows, the other baits.

A smile is a front, to show not what.
A rich man's hurt, not in a poor man's hut.
The love of life or money it may be.
For the rich man is blind, but the poor man can see.

Happiness is not a quality of all.
For each must journey down life's same hall.
We are all born rich, but in the end you see.
We all die poor, for that way it be.

JESSE WILSON

REACHING OUT

With a new frame of mind I'm reaching out.
Friends have given me a new outlook to think about.
Look to each day with a new expectation.
Think of life and love and their relation.

The pursuit of material needs.
Should be equalized by inmaterial deeds.
Do not think of a gift in terms of its material amount.
But rather the thoughts behind it that count.

Don't rush love, it will come to you.
But I can't wait much longer and I don't know what to do.
And then my friends say to me, we're all reaching out to you.
The answer to my waiting, I haven't a clue.

Feelings that I thought would never change.
Have now opened up to a wider range.
Of hearts and minds, the things needed most.
For within, self-happiness to host.

I'm thinking more now of the one up above.
The true inspiration and giver of love.
I've realized that and always will.
Thinking about his love, I am still.

Doing for others is what I live for.
But living for myself, my friends say I need to do more.
My friend says she can't make the decision.
So of my thoughts I need to make a revision.

So much to think of, so much to do.
But it's all made easier, by a friend like you.
With friends like you reaching out.
Those troubles don't seem so important to think about.

Reaching out is not a one way street.
It has to flow both ways if problems are to be beat.
So many things to think about.
That are all made easier, by just, reaching out.

I'M REACHING OUT
JESSE WILSON

SACRED FEAR

The greatest of causes for the deepest of tears.
Is the truest of all, sacred fears.
To awake in the morning with such a thought.
As to into your life what has been brought.

This is the deepest of all confronted by any.
The deepest of all dealt with by many.
To whom can you reveal this sacred fear.
With whom can you share these deepest of tears.

Is there an answer or a reply.
To this sacred fear, before I die.
There is one in whom I would like to confide.
But is this one still by my side?

JESSE WILSON

SECRET BREEZE

Over hills of emotions and through vallies of the heart.
It moves swiftly to become a part.
It flows through you with a frightening ease.
Known only as, a "Secret Breeze".

Such a mystery it does creat.
Flow with it or against it you do debate.
Will it carry you through or leave you in the air.
Does it bring with it a true falseness or a true care.

Its source is not known.
But it could be shown.
If the right person, with the right please.
Wished to discover the secret, behind the, "Secret Breeze".

DOES ANYONE WANT TO KNOW
JESSE WILSON

SHALL I CARE

If the sky should fall from perch on high.
And crumble to earth with a thunderous sigh.
Leaving the heavens an open bare.
Will I wonder, shall I care?

If the earth should fall from the grace of the sun.
Daylight no more, warmth there would be none.
With the dark and cold how would we fare?
Will I wonder, shall I care?

If the light in life does never shine.
Nor with a love, I never dine.
Be there loneliness, and companionship rare.
Will I wonder, shall I care?

If all the oceans should overflow.
And cover the earth where nothing would grow.
Sink or swim, would we dare?
Will I wonder, shall I care?

If all my life be spent alone.
Will an inner peace I have known?
If none there with me be to share.
Will I wonder, shall I care?

JESSE WILSON
I THINK I SHALL

SO FAR AWAY

Life's a road, so long it must be traveled.
Along its path are mysteries to be unraveled.
Each careful step is taken day by day.
Sometimes a peaceful rest seems so far away.

A dark narrow tunnel may be the course.
At the end of which is happiness or remorse.
At times it helps, just to stop and pray.
But the light at the end, seems to shine so far away.

Into a wide open path, life may be made.
But to keep it that way, dues must be paid.
There is no certain point at which you should stay.
Even though, where you want to be may seem so far away.

JESSE WILSON

SOFT TIS THE WORD

Soft tis the word that mourns the not.
But at such a cost this word be bought.
Soft, yet firm, this word of range.
Still yet to my heart this word is strange.

Thought twice before this word to be found.
Yet my emotions were only to be bound.
Each fair's beauty did hide her deceit.
Yet once more my heart would repeat.

The acts of the word so tenderly felt.
Yet only with cruelty and greed to be dealt.
A smile at first, turned later to a frown.
My heart uplifted only to be let down.

In some respects I've always known.
This word to exist, but as I've grown.
Seldom from fairs have I heard.
So often thought, yet soft tis the word.

JESSE WILSON

SOMEBODY PLEASE TELL ME

A feeling within my heart, please tell me.
What it is or what it shall be.
So much confusion, yet so much certainty.
So much pain to endure with reality.

I care for someone, that is why I feel.
That before my heart I am made to kneel.
To pray and plead my cry be heard.
That be understood, my unspoken word.

On the back of a picture I gave to a dream.
The words are written that I truly mean.
I have a lot going for my mind and body.
But this feeling inside, please tell me somebody.

She is at home, as am I.
Is she thinking of me, can she feel my cry?
I love her so, she makes me so happy.
Does she understand, somebody please tell me.

So much happiness I have to remember.
None dissipated by the cold of December.
Running and laughing and holding you in my arms.
Now I savor your countless charms.

The answer to me was revealed today.
By the one I care for in a special way.
You will always be my dream and my friend.
This I promise until the very end.

No one can tell me what this feeling is or what it will be.
To determine its meaning is up to me.
This feeling will always be there, and always be true.
I can tell myself now, thanks to you.

JESSE WILSON

SPANISH EYES

I feel her tremble and I hear her cries.
As I look into her tear-filled Spanish eyes.
A tight embrace that says so much.
A most wanted and needed tender touch.

A heart of gold from which emotions rise.
Can be seen through those Spanish eyes.
A shoulder if needed and a heart can be.
The most wondrous thing when given the key.

My friend I say together our hearts will last.
Joined eternally they'll withstand the past.
Ella may I ask only one thing of you?
Just hold my hand when this poem is through.

In life's circle you are among the elite.
A heart like yours will not know defeat.
Mine is with you and it hears your cries.
As I look into your Spanish eyes.

TE QUIERRO MI AMIGA. VIA CO DIOS.
JESSE WILSON

SWEET SPRING

Sweet spring is a thought as it's drawing near.
The sweet smell of flowers you hold so dear.
It changes the moods from the seasons before.
It serves as the key to unlock summer's door.

The children smile more and more each day.
The adults laugh as they watch them play.
There was once a time many years ago.
When the adults were the children laughing and playing so.

As a flower blooms so does a child.
Growing tame or growing wild.
The sweet smell of spring may not seem the same.
As when the day of adulthood from childhood came.

The air of spring has a mysterious and enchanting lure.
So sweet so clear, so sweet so pure.
It carries with it the hopes and dreams.
Of men and women, and children it seems.

The sweet smell of spring has a beauty unheard of.
Sent so abundantly and generously from the one up above.
It's as beautiful as a fair symbolized by a rose.
Can both be held, no one knows.

I wonder if the sweet smell of spring.
Can into my life happiness bring.
I've already seen a flower, but will it bloom.
I know in my heart, for it there is room.

As you look over the hills to an early sunrise.
It seems to lift up with it, many wonderful cries.
These cries can be heard in the early bird's song.
He begins it early and sings it long.

With the sweet smell of spring comes a little rain.
Also heartache and many times pain.
But the sun will rise again and the pain will ease.
And you'll feel again the wonderful uplifting sweet spring breeze.

And in the mind of an adult there does seem.
To be a rekindling of a never-dying childhood dream.
Of a long walk in the moonlight with someone by your side.
Your feelings from this flower not having to hide.

I earlier spoke of wonderful cries.
Of happiness and joys and everlasting highs.
Above all cries there seems to be.
From sweet spring a beckoning plea.

Through darkness and light you may always see.
The coming of spring and what can always be.
A joy in life that is there for the taking.
That joy is a smile on a lovely one's face making.

So clear so pure, so clean so free.
Is it true, or too good to be?
Into my life a season seems to bring.
The most wonderful thoughts of a sweet spring.

JESSE WILSON

SWEET THING

My heart was touched in a special way.
By this gift from a friend on another day.
To my heart it meant so much.
Knowing that another heart I could touch.

This friend has beauty without compare.
From her hazel eyes to her dark brown hair.
For such a friend I would do anything.
To keep near my heart the lovely "Sweet Thing".

She always has a smile and shares her joy.
Which beckons me to employ.
All my heart and all my mind.
To inspire such a friend, both lovely and kind.

Now whenever to my heart, loneliness life does bring.
I think of the one and only, most kind and lovely, "Sweet Thing".
She's there with a smile and a kind word or two.
As again she says just first love you.

Her beauty is not only on the outside.
It extends so truly to the inside.
This about her is so easy to tell.
If you know kindness and beauty you know her well.

A delightful little laugh and a cute little squeak.
Are just two small things that make her unique.
She has a way of making you feel warm.
When within your life you're enduring a storm.

Her beautiful qualities are now known well.
Over any man she could weave a spell.
It was getting to a point where I wished this life would end.
But I was lifted up by this special friend.

I can tell something about "Sweet Thing".
That to my mind thoughts do bring.
She talks to me and I to her.
Between ourselves we confer.

The one thing I wanted most.
For my writing to truly host.
Is knowing that another heart I could touch.
This means to me so very much.

Ella is she, the one that does.
Shed a brighter light, than once there was.
With so much pressure seemingly pressing down.
She can take from my face the depressing frown.

Because of friends like "Sweet Thing" I will always know.
That life will continue with its flow.
Streaming through the bright and dark days.
Searching its way through the endless maze.

Through these troubles I feel I've grown.
The reality of this world I have known.
When I think of this my mind will bring.
Thoughts of the truly, most kind and lovely "Sweet Thing".

THANKS "SWEET THING" FOR INSPIRING ME AND LETTING PART OF ME MEAN SOMETHING.
PARA ELLA
JESSE WILSON

TAKE A STEP

Take a step when it seems out of reach.
So much of a gap, one step can breach.
Have faith in yourself and take a stride.
Feelings of the heart, you should not hide.

In the morning of life, movement is a task.
But then you take a step and another you ask.
From the other side a step is taken.
A feeling of hope and your heart is shaken.

Two steps taken bring about a meeting.
Two hearts you know are hopefully beating.
A third step together and you've got it made.
To you and another, life's debt is paid.

JESSE WILSON
TAKE A STEP

THAT I MIGHT GIVE

Dear Lord I know that I continually ask.
And I know so truly you are up to the task.
I pray to you for so many things.
Yet sometimes I forget the many blessings each day brings.

JESSE WILSON

THE BEAUTIES OF THE WORLD

The beauties in the world cannot compare.
With the open heart of the lovely fair.
Her beauty is true, both outside and in.
And her open heart does attract many men.

The extent of her beauty cannot be measured.
But truly by all men should it be treasured.
The beauties of the world cannot compare.
With the open heart of a lovely fair.

JESSE WILSON

THE DARKSIDE OF LIGHT

Dawns be gone for brightness told.
Darkness is said thyself to hold.
Wandering through such ponderous ways.
Seeing the light yet in an endless maze.

Open thy mind for only to see.
The darkness within thyself and me.
Oh for true, a heart is the key.
Yet shall mine unlock the door for me.

Why may things in light be seen.
Yet others in darkness remain unseen.
A wise may says ye falter not.
Shall the mind and soul be focused ought.

Much to see there is yet to remain.
Yet still in darkness I wait in disdain.
I wonder not what the outcome might.
For all I see, is the darkness of light.

JESSE WILSON

THE FAIR

Of all the beauties in the world, the fair holds most men spellbound.
With her radiant smile and embracing glance, any man she'll astound.
No control over a man's own heart will any fair allow.
But instead, not by her own doing, she demands an everlasting vow.

From time of birth until womanhood she attains.
Her beauty and grace in all respects have made progressive gains.
From boyhood to manhood, he is ever amazed by the fair.
From her radiant smile and embracing glance, to her long golden hair.

If ever I find a lovely fair who would be by my side.
No more fears or sorrows inside my heart would I be able to hide.
To many a fair who do hold me spellbound.
Feelings for you are still around.

JESSE WILSON

THE JOINING OF OUR HANDS

My feelings inside are sometimes hard to express.
And very often it's even harder just to say yes.
Those uncertain feelings are the most difficult to understand.
But are many times made clearer by the touch of your hand.

Of your inside feelings questions you often ask.
And understanding them with you is a difficult task.
I respect those feelings, those you think about a lot.
And if ever it's needed, an open shoulder or tight embrace you've got.

Together our hearts may figure our feelings out.
But the future will always be the hardest thing to think about.
If we consider them together maybe we'll understand.
And maybe they'll be made clearer by the joining of our hands.

JESSE WILSON

THE KANDIE MAN

When you were a little girl there was always a certain joy.
Laughing and playing and hiding your thoughts about a little boy.
Your thoughts of a little boy are not often in memory's demand.
If any can bring them back, the Kandie Man can.

At times of sorrow and times of grief.
The Kandie man was there with many flavors of relief.
Drying your tears and wiping them clean.
Into your beautiful eyes bringing a gleam.

As time slowly went by.
You regarded boys with a sigh.
In your heart and in your mind.
There was a certain one, both handsome and kind.

As your beauty grows along with your heart.
From your dreams he didn't depart.
You look to the stars and the heavens that can.
Bring back to you, your Kandie Man.

The things about him you still now savor.
His smile, his laugh, his heart and its flavor.
You dwell on these things as days go by.
Apart from each other, you wonder why?

Only with your heart and a little help from above.
Will you be able to taste the Kandie Man's flavorful love.
He would gladly share it, not a penny would it cost.
You know in your heart, those feelings are not lost.

Millie, I've written of your dreams and I know that you can.
Fulfill the dreams of the Kandie Man.
I can see his heartache as the days go on.
I can see him praying that your love is not gone.

I'm a friend who cares a lot.
Who can see with certainty the love you've got.
This love of your's, believe in it you can.
Fill your life with the flavor of the Kandie Man.

BY JESSE WILSON
A FRIEND

THE LOOK OF A HEART

Tis the look of a heart yearning to be free.
Tis the look of a heart to wish I had for me.
Tis the look of a heart that is mine and your's.
Tis the look of a heart that can open life's doors.

Not worth a million no material price.
Tis the look of a heart or that such twice.
The insight of which is beyond compare.
Tis the look of a heart that should dazzle a fair.

Without an eye to provide the sight.
Tis the look of a heart that needs no light.
In the darkest of rooms in the mid of night.
Tis the look of a heart that doth shine bright.

Within itself the sight has turned.
Tis the look of a heart that sees it has yearned.
Not of certainty is what's beheld.
Tis the look of a heart that has not been befelled.

JESSE WILSON

THE SAX

A sound of meaning comes forth from the horn.
A sound of beauty from its depths is born.
With exacting motion the player acts.
To create this sound through the sax.

Ivory, brass, silver, or gold.
Throughout its history, its beauty has been told.
Many tunes through it you can play.
It can bring out the brightest in a rainy day.

The rising of the sun is accompanied by a song.
The coming of the day is brought along.
What is it about a piece?
That from life's pressures can bring a release.

A pride is felt when you hold the sax.
You dwell on its mysteries and its facts.
The early key to rock and now of jazz.
A deeper respect gained, now it has.

I have a friend who can play its song.
To perfect this art he works hard and long.
He listens to others who have mastered its keys.
He hears theirs cries through its musical pleas.

Listen closely and you may hear.
The tune he plays when he is near.
You may feel a tear and then a sigh.
Because you've heard the player's cry.

He had a look in his eye when he asked me to write.
A poem about the sax's might.
He was holding it there in his hands.
Feeling with them, its musical commands.

A clear, high note may pierce the air.
To let you know the sax is there.
Even though I cannot play.
I can listen and follow the harmonial pathway.

It can produce a song both graceful and firm.
Providing for you a definition to the terms.
Of admiration and respect.
You know not what from the sax next to expect.

Above most instruments the sax is there.
The brunt of musical messages it has to bear.
Its musical role is often subject to critique.
But all must realize the sax is unique.

The sax can be easily personified.
The one who masters its art should be exemplified.
As the player plays he seems to say.
This tune depicts life this day.

Both soothing and firm the message is clear.
In the musical harmony that you hear.
It seems to say, sit back and relax.
And listen to the music of the player and his sax.

JESSE WILSON

THE SPIRIT OF COMFORT AND RELIEF

Come the spirit of comfort and relief.
From my heart to take the grief.
The pressures of life are all around.
It seems my world is crumbling down.

Late hours of work and toil I keep.
Night after night feigning sleep.
If all this I could share with someone close to me.
I feel no more sorrows in my heart there would be.

If in the end success I achieve.
The spirit of comfort and relief, my late nights of work and toil, shall relieve.
This goal of heart and mind, I strive agonizingly to attain.
I pray to you spirit, all is not in vain.

JESSE WILSON

THE THING I LOVE MOST

None above others can bring out the emotion.
Nor hold from surging my heartfelt devotion.
At the time of greatest darkness, I see a shining light for a host.
I see none above others than the thing I love most.

Tis said in me that upcomings may try to prevent.
My long strived for and current ascent.
To the level of greatness which other hearts will host.
By none other can I attain this than the one I love most.

By way of name I need not say.
But may be looked upon each and every day.
Of none others will I ever boast.
Than the one I hold proudest, the one I love most.

JESSE WILSON

THE THINGS WE DO WHEN WE'RE IN LOVE

The things we do when we're in love.
The cries we utter to the one up above.
We give it our all, everything we've got.
But happiness in our hearts there's not.

How do we continue, how do we go on?
Another day begins with the coming of dawn.
We rise up with an inner motivation.
We don't understand it, maybe it's desperation.

The one we think of each and every day.
Seems to be going their own way.
They take with them a part of our heart.
And from our mind they never depart.

They tell me to look out and around.
They tell me of the happiness, that does there abound.
But it's very hard to see when there's so much pain.
With so much heartache nothing you gain.

I try so hard, I want to see.
The happiness they say, is there for me.
All my life, I had this dream.
In my heart it was a glowing beam.

The dream seems to be fading away.
A little more each and every day.
I can't take it, it hurts so much.
I just want to feel a soft and tender touch.

What's the matter with me, what can I do?
Without someone in my heart, I can't make it through.
Oh please someone help me with the pain.
Just a little inner happiness is all I want to gain.

The things we do when we're in love.
the cries we utter to the one up above.
Does anyone hear, does anyone care?
Does anyone want what I have to share.

JESSE WILSON
WITH LOVE

THE TIMID NEWBORN

In a lovely meadow filled with flowers and surrounded by trees.
The newborn timid creature is awed by what he sees.
Nursing at his mother, under her protection without a care.
To harm such a timid creature, what kind of predator would dare.

A scent fills the air and an alarm is sounded.
A shot rings out and the newborn is surrounded.
I got one calls a hunter, in a voice filled with glee.
He got one yells another, all come and see.

The newborn is encircled by the strange and unknown.
Room to escape, lesser and lesser has grown.
He looks to his mother in an effort to get ahead.
But all is lost, when it is realized that the source of his nursing is dead.

Here's another is said in the circle and a large blade is raised.
Another shot rings out, but this time the hunters are dazed.
From far away a voice with compassion cries.
It is meant to be another season before this newborn dies.

The newborn is alone now, in a world of confusion.
But it will not be long, until another intrusion.
To harm such a timid creature, what kind of predator can.
The answer to that as everyone knows, is man.

JESSE WILSON

THIS DAY

Of what should I say to the sorrows of this day.
But from my mind would they be away.
And from my mourning heart.
Would a lovely fair bid them depart.

They weigh so heavy now.
As to their relief, I know not how.
Would there be the slightest chance.
Of another fair, who'd my life enhance.

It may be that I should look for a shining light.
In the form of a lovely fair, with a smile so bright.
Whose open heart would my sorrows disperse.
And whose radiant beauty my thoughts would immerse.

JESSE WILSON

TIS BUT A WHISPER

Tis but a whisper, but widely heard.
Tis only a thought, an unspoken word.
Tis a spring of sorts with a hidden source.
Flow forth from not regret nor remorse.

Trickle down, but yet not a drop heard.
With each ripple in the pool, another unspoken word.
As the waves spread out so does the word.
But still as yet it has not been heard.

Tis but a whisper until given voice.
To be heard is a better choice.
Not only when spoken does a word take effect.
Takes but a whisper for action to perfect.

JESSE WILSON

TIS SAID THE END

Tis said the end to be at which.
When the heart and mind are in a nervous twitch.
For which the cause be not known.
The end to others seems to be shown.

110

Gone are reasons for caring and love.
The most to be shown by the one up above.
Is there one to cause lost's return.
Or is the end of the rope forever to burn.

JESSE WILSON

TIS THERE MEANING

Tis there meaning in the heart, behind lock and key.
Reveal it or not for there it may be.
Two sides at odds, opposing each other.
One has the key, one has the other.

Two sides at odds, opposing each other.
Victory or defeat, for one another.
Two sides wage war within a whole.
A battle rages forth within a soul.

One side says yes, the other says no.
Happiness to one the other can show.
Happiness is desired, but not at the cost.
Of a love bound friendship painfully lost.

The battle thus spoke of is raging inside.
A battered heart still trying to hide.
The key to one, the other will not give.
For if it did, I could not forgive.

Could never forgive nor ever forget.
But would I live with friendship or regret.
Other hearts involved have not been told.
For I could not forgive, so shall I withhold.

Tis there meaning behind lock and key.
The answer is yes, for there it may be.
How long behind lock will it stay.
Forever or a moment is not known this day.

JESSE WILSON
I COULD NOT FORGIVE ONE SIDE OF ME FOR DAMNING THE OTHER COULD ANYONE ELSE?

TO BE NOT SINCERE

To be not sincere to me.
Tis to be not sincere to the.
A quality not lost, but hard to find.
A quality of the heart, one of a kind.

Who am I to speak of this.
No one seems to know, but would they miss.
I know myself, inside me it is there.
I want so much, it only to share.

I've seen very few others who could honestly say.
That to you they would be sincere by the end of the day.
I feel I've been hurt, something taken away.
Very few words to help, could you say.

I've been sincere to the maximum for the.
Is it wrong to ask the same for me.
At your wish, I'm there when needed.
Your cries and joys I've always heeded.

I remember a time when each other we did not know.
But the likeness of our hearts was soon to show.
Somehow I knew I could confide in you.
As I've done before with very few.

A song about you I have on my mind.
My sunrise in the morning so beautiful and kind.
A sunrise in the morning, what a sight to see.
But not as pretty as the, but not as pretty as the.

Sincerity to the, what does it mean.
Sincerity to me, creates its own scene.
To be not sincere to me.
Tis to be not sincere to the.

YO SOY UN HOMBRE SINCERO
JESSE WILSON

TO LEAD THE LOT

One among others rises to have what is sought.
The strength and ability to lead the lot.
He is the first one out and the last one in.
Always willing after the end, to begin.

This one among others has assumed a spot.
Atop of the mountain to lead the lot.
Direction and guidance he must give.
For in order a full life, the lot to live.

Long days grow longer and duties more.
And the day does not end with the closing of the door.
Out into the world to find the strays.
Traveling the road through endless days.

JESSE WILSON

TOO SAD IS THE HEART THAT WALKS ALONE

To sad is the heart that walks alone.
Captive emotions within do roam.
Their expression if gained, would ease the pain.
Of the heart that walks alone.

Inside a young man with ambitious desires.
Lie the dwindling coals of emotion's fires.
Their meaning and importance, how long shall they remain unknown?
Too sad is the heart that walks alone.

JESSE WILSON

TORN FROM THE DAY

Torn from the scorn of day is brightness.
Of the spirit be it the likeness.
Which befalleth the lonely soul.
Pursuith the treasure as goal.

Wait for that in which there is worth.
Bring it forth and guide it to thine hearth.
Tender it care and give it joy.
Bring forth from thine heart the truth and not a ploy.

Arise in the morning with a body of glow.
the comings of the day for to show.
The beauty of that which is a fair.
Revealith the truth and tender it care.

I seek ye desires with emotion it's true.
These emotions I give again anew.
A wish I've made and for it I long.
Receiveth or not I pray my soul remains strong.

Torn from the scorn of day is brightness.
Of the spirit be it the likeness.
Which befalleth the lonely soul.
And gain the treasure of which is a goal.

MAY A WISH FROM THE DAY COME TRUE
JESSE WILSON

TRUE TO YOU, TRUE TO ME

My dearest of friends, I've often thought.
Of the many joys to me you've brought.
Of the many good times and the many tears.
Seems like a friendship that will last for years.

You put your arms around me and you give me your love.
I see in you a mission sent from up above.
Everything I've always wanted, always wanted to be.
Is here, because I am true to you and you are true to me.

So many thoughts from which to choose.
A solution to each is there to use.
The only one that seems to be.
Is the one that lies the deepest, the deepest within me.

We speak of our problems in all honesty.
And it is because of this that I will still be true to you and you true to me.
I've held your hand when you wanted to cry.
Because you felt a part of you was about to die.

You held me close as I let the tears flow.
I let it all out, I let it go.
You almost left me then, but something inside.
Told you to stay, to stay by my side.

To stay by my side, I know is asking a lot.
But it doesn't measure up against what I've got.
I've got a heart in which caring will never end.
Caring will never end, never end for you my friend.

Where do hearts join and where do they part?
Never an ending, but always a start.
You said a habit of your's is forgiveness for all.
But on it, can the dearest of friends make a call?

On what is friendship based?
Unless with it the truth is faced.
To run from it, would not bring relief.
But only from behind, a greater grief.

I've written before of your Spanish eyes.
I've written before of hearing your cries.
I've written before of what I wanted to be.
Because I am true to you and you are true to me.

JESSE WILSON
TRUE TO EACH OTHER

TWICE GONE BY

Two times have past, ten years in each.
Lessons to learn and lessons to teach.
Many undecided, few are sloved.
At this mark in life, twenty years resolved.

Twice gone by, two measures of life.
A dime wished for each time of struggle and strife.
Tears of joy and pains of sorrow.
Each day I wondered what will come tomorrow.
A boy at heart I will always be.
A man of mind in the future I see.

A first attempt at life not a total success.
Personal fault and others I readily confess.
Mistakes to make I know there are more.
But with the keys of success I will open life's doors.

Twenty years ahead I pray to be.
The person I desire, the true and real me.
And when the Lord calls for me to live on high.
Two measures of life will have twice gone by.

JESSE WILSON

WHAT I KNOW

For I know so little Lord of what you have to say.
I yearn to know more each and every day.
Like an impatient child, sometimes I charge ahead.
Listening to you would be so much wiser instead.

The chance you have given Lord, is so grand and true.
Brothers and sisters it is given to me and you.
Your children afar are brought closer this day.
To be a guide to them so much we pray.

I thank you Lord for the love you have shown.
For the feeling in me, that during this time has grown.
For I know now Lord, just a little bit more.
In thy son's name, we trust and adore.

JESSE WILSON
"IN CHRIST'S NAME"

WHAT I NEED

Everyone says they know what I need.
But my cries they rarely heed.
I cry so loud but do they hear.
Into my eye comes a tear.

Too sad is the heart that walks alone.
I know this is true because mine is on its own.
A need, a want, a desire yes it's true.
To be happy, not to be blue.

A smooth soft hand and a tender touch.
To me means so much.
As I look into her eyes.
I pray to the one above the skies.

Everyone says they know what I need.
But my cries they rarely heed.
I cry so loud but do they hear.
Into my eye comes a tear.

JESSE WILSON
SUNSHINE AND RAIN, HEARTACHE AND PAIN
FROM THESE THINGS I NEED TO GAIN

WHY

The oldest question we ask each other is why?
Why do we laugh and why do we cry?
Is there an answer to this question we ask?
Or is finding it an impossible task?

Why do we hurt each other as we often do?
Why is there heartache for me and for you?
Why does Mom fight with Dad?
Is there a difference between the good and the bad.

Why do the world's nations hate each other?
Why can't we consider each man our brother?
Why are people different because of what they believe?
Why, as to the truth, do we each other deceive?

Why don't people understand?
That there can be truth in a helping hand?
Why can't we reach out and take that hand?
Are we afraid of a hidden demand?

Why is there sunshine and why is there rain?
Why is there heartache and why is there pain?
Why can't we be happier more often than not?
Why not put our will to be so, on the spot?

Why do we feel we have lost?
When it is up to us to determine the cost?
Why can't we rise above the ground?
When we feel that love is not around?

Why do little boys play so rough?
Why is it important for us macho guys to seem so tough?
Why do we surround ourselves with an outer shell?
While putting ourselves through an internal hell?

Why do we live and why do we die?
Why is there blue in the sky?
Why are we kind and why are we cruel?
Why do we, with our emotions, wage a duel?

Why does it matter who's wrong or right?
Why does deciding cause friends to fight?
Why can't we on our emotions get a grip?
Why don't we understand the most important thing is friendship?

Why do we struggle and why do we strive?
Why do we keep painful dreams alive?
Why do such things bring a guy and girl together?
Why do feelings change as quickly as the weather?

Why do I hurt, but yet still care?
Why do I with others still want to share?
Why do you hurt so much?
Why do you still reach out for a tender touch?

Why can't I help you with your heartache?
Why can't, from my heart, the sorrows you take?
Why is the answer to this question the same as it always was?
Why is the answer to this question still, because?

JESSE WILSON

WIN OR LOSE

Crying out, a body screams with pain.
From within you feel energy drain.
Everyone must pay their dues.
Whether you win or whether you lose.

Life is the same, even though it's not a sport.
You live your days out on a more open court.
Points are scored and points are stopped.
Win or lose a goal you've topped.

If you give it your all, nothing is lost.
Realistically you determine the cost.
Everyone has to pay their dues.
Whether you win or whether you lose.

JESSE WILSON

YOUTH

Youth is a quality above all others desired.
Leadership is an ability which must be acquired.
Through good times and bad.
Both can be had.

Persistence and drive are needed most.
For inside your heart these qualities to host.
You all have these qualities to an undefinable end.
This experience will always be remembered, especially between friends.

JESSE WILSON